The Book of

THE BOOK OF DECISION

Published by Arcturus Publishing Limited,
1-7 Shand Street, London SE1 2ES.

First published 2001.
This edition printed 2002.

©Text The School of Economic Science.
©Design Arcturus Publishing Limited.

Typeset by Christopher Smith Design.
Printed in China.

The Book of

Introduction

'Decision' is the second of three books devoted to making philosophical ideas practical. It concerns a central issue in our lives: the decisions we make.

Some of our choices seem to be of no great consequence, while others are vital and may deeply affect ourselves and all those around us, but regardless of their relative importance, all our decisions have their effect.

This book is devoted to developing a more rational approach to life by encouraging a conscious reference to our primary basis of judgement, our source of inner consciousness, the light of Reason itself. Through practice and reflection it develops 'the gentle art of unity', and by so doing shifts our system of choice away from those things which can do nothing but limit our freedom and hold us in isolation, towards an ever widening integration and understanding.

Divided into twelve stages, with seven reflections for each stage, 'Decision' provides a day by day programme to support the course of practical philosophy from which it arose. Although derived from those classes, what is to be found in this book provides insight and inspiration for all.

Use it as a practical tool. Carry it with you and refer to it regularly. Whatever you face in life, what is to be found in 'Decision' is of immense and immediate benefit.

If you wish to discover more about practical philosophy telephone The School of Economic Science on 0207 835 1256

Finding peace in the present

At the heart of these twelve stages in the development of a more reflective attitude to life is a simple and yet powerful practice. This practice allows you not only to connect fully with all those demands that life continually lays upon you, but also to reflect the still light of consciousness which illuminates it all.

The practice can be undertaken anywhere and at any time regardless of your circumstances, at times of quiet and in the midst of action. It can be practised for any length of time, for two minutes or more. Even a single moment has its merit.

Come into the present by leaving concerns for past and future. Fall still, and let go all physical tension. Connect mind with the senses.

And be aware of the beauty around you.
See colour and form. Let listening be wide.
Go beyond the surface of sensory impression.
Become conscious of the underlying silence and space.

Rest in the peace of the present.

And then, having found rest, move on to the next activity, meeting the moment, moment by moment.

Stage One

The gentle art of unity

The soul attains her perfectly rounded form when she is neither straining out after something nor shrinking back; neither disseminating herself piecemeal nor yet sinking down in collapse but is bathed in a radiance which reveals to her the world and herself in their true colours.

MEDITATIONS MARCUS AURELIUS

1. *Resist cramming.*
When you become jammed into a corner
desperate for time and space, afford time to
rest within to discover that inner space which
will allow you to act effectively.

2. *Consciousness illuminates everything that comes before the mind. Rather than being continually identified with all that is lit, use the Practice to rest in the consciousness itself.*

3. *Although we attempt to improve our outer circumstances, it is our subtle inner qualities which are the most important things, for they colour everything we experience. Find true satisfaction by turning in..*

4. *The mind is forever reaching out or sinking back. Return to the quiet appreciation of beauty to establish harmony and balance.*

5. *'The still mind finds happiness in everything.
The kingdom within is the reservoir of peace and bliss.'*

Hold these sentences before the mind. Return to
them again and again.

6. Throw yourself into life with enthusiasm, but try to avoid claiming everything as your own private possession.

7. *It's impossible to love in isolation. The consciousness that illuminates the individual mind illuminates everything. Look there for true happiness.*

Stage Two

Remembering the reality

We have come into the world for the sake of discovering joy. But instead we have fallen into the trap of ignorance. Ignorance is forgetting the reality. It is the cause of all the trouble associated with the world. Therefore the biggest of all the troubles is to forget the reality.

GOOD COMPANY SHANTANANDA SARASWATI

1. *To act outside habit is a true test of intention. To change the habits of mind requires a degree of determination. When you find yourself falling back into the usual modes of thinking and acting adopt a determined approach.*

2. At the heart of philosophical living lies the search for knowledge, for happiness and a greater fullness of life. All these require open mindedness and open heartedness. If you find the mode of thinking you have adopted at present doesn't require these, check its validity.

3. *To adopt an evolutionary approach, seek the harmonizing factor in every situation you meet.*

4. *If you find discord and division figures largely in your life, look out for mistaken thinking which confuses fleeting pleasure for lasting happiness, shallow cleverness for profound understanding, constant activity for true satisfaction.*

5. Work for inner contentment and stability regardless
of the circumstances you meet. Real wealth lies within.
Seek there to escape poverty.

6.

DISCRIMINATION → DECISION → CREATION

| The basis of our choices | → | The nature of our choices | → | The result of our choices |

Consider the nature of the choices you make regardless of their apparent importance. Observe the basis upon which these choices are made. Consider the effect of these choices and what is created by them.

7. *Have recourse to reason through the Practice of Finding Peace in the Present. Notice the effect this has on your choices and what results from those choices.*

Stage Three

Witness

As long as the concept 'me and mine and thee
and thine' crowd the show, the conscious witness
in the background remains unavailed.
Only witness avails freedom, whereas claimant
looks for the object of claim.

SHANTANANDA SARASWATI

1. *The law of entropy states that in time everything must inevitably run down. We are subject to this law. Conscious effort is the only thing that will halt a decline in consciousness. We cannot stand still. Sustain your efforts.*

2. *By making conscious efforts we rise above habit. There is a dividing line. On one side lies the habitual, on the other the conscious. Cross the line and life evolves. There we discover an increased awareness of our own true stature.*

3.

Each time we practise one of our habits, that habit is reinforced. Likewise every time we make a conscious effort to step free, that habit is weakened.

4.

By breaking through the confines of habit the light of
reason has the opportunity to inform our contribution to life.

5. A most powerful habit is the habit of self forgetting. Forgetting is caused by binding ourselves by claim. When you find your claims possessing you, enjoy the power you truly possess by recourse to consciousness.

6. *If your intention is to ascend in consciousness and live a more rational life, be reflective. Find time to retire even for a few moments rather than be subject to the onward thrust of life which compels us all to move from identification to identification.*

7. *We all have our habitual way of meeting events, and events of themselves have a mechanical way of repeating themselves until recourse to consciousness offers an alternative.*

Stage Four

The simple solution

Pulchritudo splendor veritatis.
Beauty is the splendour of truth.
Simplex sigillum veri.
The simple is the seal of the true.

LATIN MOTTOES

1. *If truth is our aim, value things for their beauty and simplicity.*

2. *Shifts of mood continually take place. Very often we think that they are caused by something beyond us, but if we find that we are meeting the same old situation in the same old way, look for those clusters of thoughts and emotions that we have somehow adopted and made our own.*

3. *May thoughts and feelings be less private than we first imagine? May we be influenced by a general state of heart and mind?*
Look out for undercurrents of negative emotion, and when it would seem that they are drawing you down, withdraw your belief from their effects.

4. *Remember that even the darkest shadow is cast by light. Rather than living in the shadows look to the light.*

5. *The forms of creation have a consuming interest, and the more we are enlivened the more fascinating everything appears. Enjoy to the full all that you are offered, but never forget the light of consciousness that empowers your appreciation.*

6. If our experience of life is lacking in vitality, rise above that which ensnares heart and mind, and allow the vitality within to unite with the vitality that surrounds us everywhere.

7. Notice the inevitable effect of the company we keep. Seek the best company, and this goes for the thoughts and feelings we entertain as well as those things that come our way in the outer circumstances of life.

Stage Five

_____

In the spirit of service

Once a king invited everyone for a feast. He laid down particular rules for this particular occasion. Everyone was asked to put on a bamboo jacket. Having put on the jacket the hand could not be brought to the mouth, making eating impossible. Having gone to each table in turn and witnessed people's difficulty, he finally came to the table where the wise were seated. They were also dressed in bamboo jackets. They had found a way out. Instead of feeding themselves, they fed each other and thereby enjoyed the feast. Having seen the trick, everyone learnt how to enjoy the feast.

TRADITIONAL TEACHING STORY

1. *There is the observer and the objects of observations. Those objects, physical and subtle, must lie beyond us. If they do, we cannot be them. It is the conscious witness, not those things with which we readily identify, who is at the heart of who we really are.*

2. Are all our concerns of lasting significance or matters which are, though demanding of attention, bound to come to pass?

3. *Free yourself from turgid emotion and arid intellectualisation. Develop instead a light touch, by continually refreshing yourself at the source of all that is genuinely heart felt and truly intelligent.*

4. *The mark of the discerning thought and deed is simplicity and beauty. Resting in the conscious witness allows for simplicity and beauty to be expressed in all that we do.*

5. *The effect of negative emotion is always debilitating. Avoid giving way to it. Consciousness, the source of all vitality, when fueling negation creates the opposite - debility.*

6. By giving our attention to anything, there is inevitably an act of service. In developing a discriminating approach to life, we begin to identify and evaluate the things we serve. Learn how to keep the very best of company in the spirit of service.

7. *If you seem to suffer from deprivation in your life, take an honest look at where your mind is going and the company you are keeping. If you are merely serving some narrow claim, remember the men in their bamboo jackets and turn out, and serve the person opposite. Without being too concerned about the result, simply make the offering.*

Stage Six

Perfect freedom

The author of peace and lover of concord,
in knowledge of whom standeth our eternal life,
whose service is perfect freedom.

BOOK OF COMMON PRAYER

1. *If our aim is perfect freedom, consciously serve peace and concord by stepping away from trivial concerns and petty aggravations, turning instead to inner stillness.*

2. *Bound by concerns and involvements, some so deep rooted they remain unrecognised, there would appear to be little chance to become the lover of peace and concord. We can only begin to make a move in this direction by conscious connection and simple service.*

3. *Before launching into action refer to reason.*
How is my soul's helmsman going about his task?
Reason is the helmsman of the soul. The soul under
reason finds freedom.

4. *The future never comes. Our only opportunity is now. If bound by the confines of heart and mind, don't wait for a more opportune time. There is only one opportunity and only one time.*

5. *Give yourself the opportunity to shine. By constant recourse to the Practice step free of agitation and lethargy. Find that in the process you will give others opportunities of their own.*

6. *Consider those patterns of mind that are life-enhancing and those that are energy debilitating. Ask yourself what you are encouraging at present and what effect that has on those around you.*

7. For the individual to evolve, for society to evolve, we must seek to change the balance of our lives.
The speed at which that evolution takes place is dependent upon the decisions we make. The quality of those decisions is dependent on the degree of consciousness we bring to them. Regardless of the confines we face remember the source of perfect freedom.

Stage Seven

True happiness

The laughter of the gods must be defined to be their exuberant energy in the universe, and the cause of gladness of all mundane creatures.

'PLATONIC POLITICS' PROCLUS

1. 'Exuberance' and 'gladness' are not discovered dashing about, exhausting ourselves searching for an elusive happiness to be found out there somewhere. The true philosophers, whoever they are, wherever they exist, turn within to find the source of gladness.

2. *The reason why it is possible to connect with the world of the gods rather than believing ourselves to be mundane creatures is because the gods exist within us. They embody the principles of knowledge consciousness and bliss.*

3. *Why live a mundane existence when heaven is laid out on the face of the earth? Cast aside confining concern and look.*

4. *In truth are things really so mundane? The real question we should be posing ourselves is: 'Why are things that are by nature so profoundly beautiful dismissed as being merely mundane?'*

5. *The course that reason dictates is away from the materialisation of events towards that source of energy from which they arise. This involves not merely reacting to whatever life throws at us, but connecting with the source of things, the home of true vitality. It involves learning to live life creatively, empowered by that vitality rather than being constantly on the receiving end.*

6. *The mark of any great work of art is the aura that surrounds it, a power that transcends its obvious limitations. We should attempt the same thing in our own lives, playing our parts so fully and so beautifully that we transcend our limits.*

7. *Any insight we might have gained inevitably drifts away from us if we fail to formulate our thoughts. Without conscious thought and clear formulation habit will inevitably rule. Habit obliterates perception.*

Stage Eight

From the partial to the whole

And thou shouldst know that all have their delight
in measure as their sight sinketh more deep into
the truth wherein every intellect is stilled.

'PARADISO' XXVIII, 106 DANTE

I. Be aware of partial vision. In the normal run of events we can only see things from 'my point of view'. This point of view is circumscribed by my partialities: the ideas I am partial to, the feelings I am partial to, the desires I am partial to. To all of these we have lent our identity, and being partial it is only part of the story. Widen the mind to new possibility.

2. *The more we are partial to, the more we dismiss. The more we dismiss, the more we become isolated from the whole. What in the end we are left with might not amount to very much, but at least we have control over our small corner, or so we try to convince ourselves - despite the evidence to the contrary.*

3. *By turning within expand your view. By so doing develop a keener sense of measure by acting appropriately in accordance with what the situation really demands.*

4. *Contained in the passing flow of events are all the things that happen to us, all the people we meet, all the influences that come to bear upon us, and in response to this flow we seek our identity. As all these things are constantly changing so must the sense we have of ourselves.*

5. *First rest in the consciousness within, and then turn out to meet the passing flow with a sense of rest and depth. This is how to bring clarity to the mind and lightness of thought and feeling to everything we meet.*

6. We *cannot possess the truth but we can allow it to operate through us.*

7. There is no loss of identity in this process, quite the contrary. Our role in life, like everything else that comes before the mind, is invested with a new depth of understanding.

Stage Nine

The third factor

The soul should collect and concentrate itself in its Self.
'PHAEDO' – PLATO

There are two natures, one self-existent,
and the other ever in want.
'PHILEBUS' – PLATO

May the outward and the inward man be at one.
'PHAEDRUS' – PLATO

1. *Follow this process:*

Step One: *Allow the body to relax.*
Step Two: *Still the mind by coming into the present.*
Step Three: *Become aware of consciousness*
                  illuminating the mind.
Step Four: *Retain that awareness when meeting*
                  needs as they arise.

2. *The choice is between revolution, repeating the same old habit, or evolution, coming into an ever closer accord with who we truly are.*

SION

3. Even though we might be as rich as Croesus, by acquiring the wrong set of riches we may still die in want. This is a sad kind of poverty but much sought after. Avoid becoming possessed by your possessions. But turn instead to the one possession where this can never be a danger: consciousness itself, the root of all wisdom, the source of life itself.

4. *When there is full connection both with the world around us and the illuminating light of consciousness, there is little wonder that our impressions are so bright and vivid. Seek that connection now, not at some other time.*

5. *The fabric of your life is formed in the relationship between you and the flow of events. It is woven of desire and aversion. Both draw heavily on human vitality. When feeling worn out notice the effect of these two.*

6. 'Me' and the passing flow of events are two inconstants trying to form a relationship. It's the third factor which creates harmony between the two, and depth of understanding. The Practice encourages the growth of that third factor.

7. *If when addressing the complications of life we remember the underlying simplicity of consciousness, it is possible to discover the true measure of any situation. What do we mean by the true measure? That which perfectly meets the need. This is undoubtedly practical wisdom.*

Stage Ten

Conscious connection

Men who are foolish and ignorant are careless and never watchful; but the man who lives in watchfulness considers it his greatest joy.

'DHAMMAPADA' VERSE 26 BUDDHA

1. *If you feel that life is passing you by, remember that you are the witness of life. Discover the joy in simply observing what is there.*

2. Notice the operation of random and inconsequential thought. When you see it in operation don't be unduly concerned. Instead, go back to the practice of simple attention.

3. Break through the barrier of circling thought by continually letting go and constantly connecting. Circling thoughts engross the mind whilst conscious connection enlivens it.

4. And don't add to your stock of circling thoughts with feelings of helplessness. Make connection instead, first within through the Practice and then without through precise attention.

5. The real source of satisfaction is not to be found in yet more material possessions, but only in a deeper and more profound experience of life. This can only be achieved by disciplining the mind and opening the heart.

6. *And when embracing the situations you meet, allow the need to create the measure. Do and say nothing more than the situation demands. This is the elegant solution.*

7. Consider what is natural and what is strained about your life, what is nourishing and what is of less value. If you find you have made the wrong decision avoid self criticism. Instead learn and resolve.

Stage Eleven

Informed by reason

Where there is hate, let me bring Love –
Where there is offence, let me bring Pardon –
Where there is discord, let me bring Union –
Where there is error, let me bring Truth –
Where there darkness, let me bring Light.

THE PRAYER OF SAINT FRANCIS

I. *The free flow of the BEAUTIFUL from the BEAUTIFUL to the BEAUTIFUL purifies the SOUL.*

Without trying to work it out, simply hold this thought in mind.

2. *If we are to live a full and useful life, there will inevitably be constant demands put upon us. We need to be able to meet them effectively and responsibly. Responsibility means simply the ability to respond - to respond fully and effectively in a way that is exactly measured to the need.*

3. *The measured response to need is a sure indication of practical wisdom. There is a certainty about it, a feeling of rightness. The same words and the same actions might be entirely wrong at another time and in another place, but for this time, in this place, these words and deeds, informed by reason, resolve the situation, or at least they make it possible to move towards a resolution. Anything other than this measured response will tend to divide.*

4. *Reason integrates, harmonises, and resolves difference because it is derived directly from the principle of unity. When we talk about many reasons for doing something those reasons are all derived from and go to serve the one unifying factor (that is when they are genuine reasons and not merely justifications for being unreasonable). Reason always relates to unity. Act from reason not justification.*

5. *'The flight from the alone to the Alone.'*

Consider whether the decisions you make are serving the separate self or constitute a movement towards the greater whole.

6. Alone is derived from all one. Appreciate the unity of life; encourage connection in all that you meet, and in the process step out of loneliness and isolation.

7. The major thing that keeps us in a state of separation is all those ideas we hold about ourselves. Although they often contradict each other, they have one thing in common. None of them are true. But when they hold sway over the mind, they certainly have their effect. When these usurpers rise and take power don't try to battle it out, simply return to the light of reason.

Stage Twelve

Live consciously

Our deeper feelings are not of ourselves alone,
but are glimpses of a reality transcending the
narrow limits of our particular consciousness -
that the harmony and beauty of the face of
Nature is at root one with the gladness that
transfigures the face of man.

'SCIENCE AND THE UNSEEN WORLD'
SIR ARTHUR EDDINGTON

1. *Remember these words of profound reason: 'It is in giving oneself that one receives; it is in forgetting oneself that one is found.'*

2. *Discover a new understanding by stepping over the usual constraints. By discarding the limited and by embracing the whole, discover that in essence love and reason are the same thing.*

3. *There is no room in any of this for self righteous claim. Reason has its own way of operating. Simply become the vehicle.*

4. *A philosophical frame of mind is a civilized frame of mind, the mark of the truly humane. Consider in what way, large or small, you might serve the philosophical purpose in what life is offering now.*

5. *Humanity is bound by a common bond. In experience that bond is achieved not so much through the eradication of the differences, but by allowing those differences to connect with their common source. Constantly seek the common source, both in yourself and in those you meet.*

6. *There is a general desire to experience greater depth and happiness, but depth and happiness do not come by chance but only by developing a frame of mind that will encourage their presence.*

7. We can never experience depth of happiness and understanding in isolation. When the mind becomes still and reflective what we are experiencing is a reality which goes beyond any self imposed limits.
Be reflective. Use reason. Live consciously.

Final Thought

Flexible, intelligent creative, true: these are qualities much valued and rightly so. They are the qualities possessed by those that can connnect with their own core of consciousness, the light of reason itself.

Conclusion

*The decisions we make create
the life we lead.*

Why make the wrong decisions?

*The reflections found in this book
will help you rise above the common
confines and live in the
light of reason.*